A Day in the Life: Sea Animals

Turtle

Louise Spilsbury

www.raintreepublishers.co.uk
Visit our website to find out
more information about
Raintree books.

To order:
☎ Phone 0845 6044371
▤ Fax +44 (0) 1865 312263
▧ Email myorders@raintreepublishers.co.uk

Customers from outside the UK please telephone +44 1865 312262

Raintree is an imprint of Capstone Global Library Limited,
a company incorporated in England and Wales having
its registered office at 7 Pilgrim Street, London, EC4V 6LB
– Registered company number: 6695582

Text © Capstone Global Library Limited 2011
First published in hardback in 2011
First published in paperback in 2012
The moral rights of the proprietor have been asserted.

Edited by Sian Smith, Nancy Dickmann, and Rebecca Rissman
Designed by Joanna Hinton-Malivoire
Picture research by Mica Brancic
Production by Victoria Fitzgerald
Originated by Capstone Global Library Ltd
Printed and bound in China by South China Printing
Company Ltd

ISBN 978 1 4062 1705 6 (hardback)
14 13 12 11 10
10 9 8 7 6 5 4 3 2 1

ISBN 978 1 4062 1889 3 (paperback)
15 14 13 12 11
10 9 8 7 6 5 4 3 2 1

**British Library Cataloguing in Publication
Data**
Spilsbury, Louise.
  Turtle. -- (A day in the life. Sea animals)
  1. Sea turtles--Pictorial works--Juvenile literature.
  I. Title II. Series
  597.9'28-dc22

Acknowledgements
We would like to thank the following for permission to
reproduce photographs: Alamy pp.5, 22 (© Michael Patrick
O'Neill), 8, 23: flipper (© Anthony Grote); FLPA p.15 (Peter
Reynolds); Getty Images pp.12 (Heinrich van den Berg), 13
(Photonica/Michael Duva); Image Quest Marine pp.6 (V&W/
Mark Conlin), 9, 23: surface (Masa Ushioda), 7, 10, 23:
breathe (Soren Edgeberg), 11 (Andre Seale); Photolibrary pp.4
(age fotostock/Michael S Nolan), 14 (Tips Italia/Reinhard
Dirscherl), 16 (Animals Animals/George HH. Huey), 17,
18, 23: female, 23: hatch (Oxford Scientific Films (OSF)/
Olivier Grunewald), 19 (All Canada Photos/Wayne Lynch),
20 (Waterframe - Underwater Images/Ethan Daniels), 21
(Waterframe - Underwater Images/Masa Ushioda).

Cover photograph of a hawksbill turtle swimming above a
reef reproduced with permission of Corbis (© Paul Souders).
Back cover photograph of eggs reproduced with permission of
Photolibrary (Oxford Scientific Films (OSF)/Olivier Grunewald).
Back cover photograph of flippers reproduced with permission
of Alamy (© Anthony Grote).

We would like to thank Michael Bright for his invaluable help
in the preparation of this book.

Contents

What is a turtle? 4
What do turtles look like? 6
What do turtles do all day? 8
How do turtles swim? 10
What do turtles do at night? 12
How do turtles catch food? 14
Where do turtles lay their eggs? 16
What are turtle babies like? 18
What hunts turtles? 20
Turtle body map 22
Glossary 23
Find out more 24
Index 24

Some words are shown in bold, **like this**.
You can find them in the glossary on page 23.

green turtle

Turtles are animals that live in the ocean.

Some turtles stay close to land and others swim far across the oceans.

leatherback turtle

There are lots of different types of turtles.

The leatherback turtle can grow longer than a motorbike.

shell

leatherback turtle

Turtles have shells on their backs.

Most turtles have hard shells but leatherback turtles have rubbery shells.

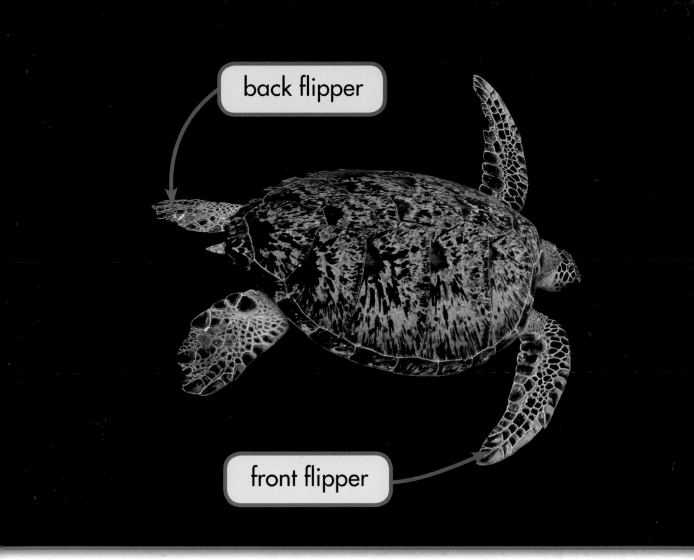

back flipper

front flipper

All turtles have two front **flippers** and two back flippers.

Turtles cannot pull their head or flippers back into their shell like tortoises.

W__t __ t__rtl__ d__ all day?

Most turtles spend a lot of time swimming during the day.

They swim near the **surface** of the ocean in the day and deeper at night.

Turtles swim across oceans to find places to lay their eggs and to find food.

Some turtles rest for short times in the afternoon.

front flippers

Turtles use their large front **flippers** like paddles to pull them forwards.

They use their back flippers to help them steer.

Turtles use their strong front flippers to dive deep underwater.

They have to come to the **surface** to **breathe** again.

What do turtles do at night?

Female turtles lay their eggs on land at night.

During the night turtles spend some time looking for food in the ocean.

Turtles can see and smell very well underwater.

Turtles use these **senses** to help them find food when it is dark.

How do turtle catch food?

jellyfish

Turtles have a mouth without any teeth that is shaped a bit like a bird's beak.

Some turtles catch jellyfish by grabbing them with this strong beak.

spines

Inside a leatherback turtle's mouth and throat there are lots of sharp spines.

These spines stop slippery jellyfish escaping from the leatherback's mouth.

Where do turtles lay their eggs?

Every two to three years, a **female** turtle crawls onto a beach at night to lay eggs.

Most turtles swim a long way to find the same beach they were born on.

Female turtles dig holes in the sand with their back **flippers**.

They lay eggs in the holes and then push sand over the eggs to hide them.

W --t --r t--rtl babies like?

egg

Baby leatherback turtles are black.

The babies **hatch** from eggs under the sand and climb out of the nest at night.

The babies crawl down the beach towards the sea.

They move in the dark to hide from animals that hunt them on land.

lizard

Dogs, lizards, birds, and crabs hunt baby turtles when they crawl to the sea.

In the sea, octopuses, sharks, and other large fish hunt baby turtles.

20

shark

Sharks and killer whales hunt adult leatherback turtles.

Adult turtles can swim fast and their shells are too tough for many animals.

Turtle body map

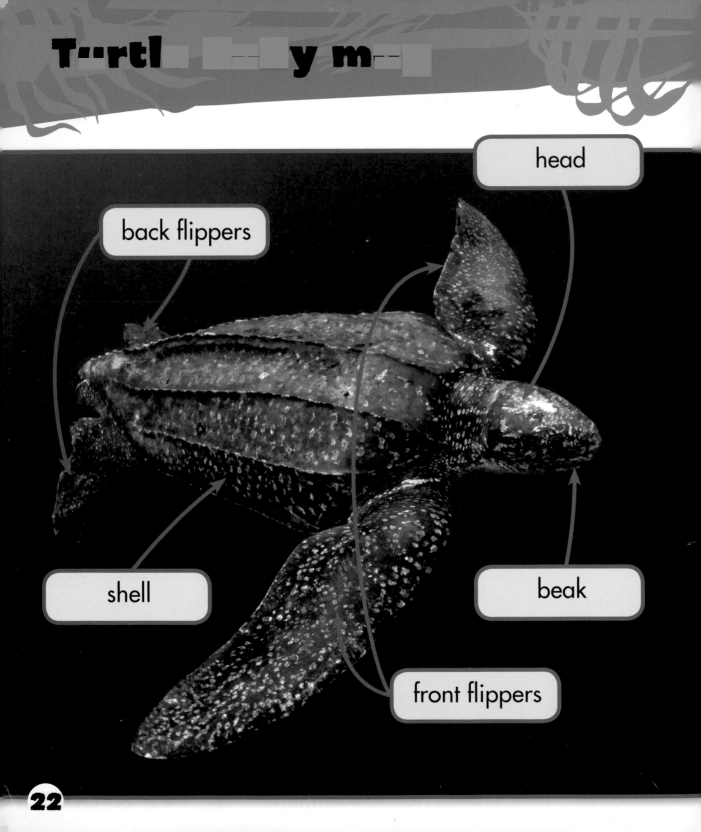

head

back flippers

shell

beak

front flippers

breathe to take air into the body

female animal that can lay eggs or have babies

flipper flat part of a turtle's body that it uses for swimming

hatch when a baby animal comes out of its egg

senses powers that animals use to find out about the world around them, such as sight and hearing

surface top of the sea

Fi... ...t m..r

Books

Sea Turtles (Undersea Encounters), Mary Jo Rhodes and David Hall (Children's Press, 2006)

The Life of a Sea Turtle (Life Cycles), Clare Hibbert (Raintree Publishers, 2005)

Websites

Watch a video on leatherback turtles at: **kids.nationalgeographic.com/Animals/CreatureFeature/Leatherback-sea-turtle**

Find out all about turtles including their senses and what they eat at: **www.seaworld.org/animal-info/info-books/sea-turtle/index.htm**

Index

babies 18, 19, 20
beak 14, 22
breathing 11
eggs 9, 12, 16, 17, 18
feeding 9, 14, 15
flipper 7, 10, 17, 22
hunting 12, 13, 14, 15

movement 10, 11, 16, 18, 19
resting 9
senses 13
shell 6, 7, 21, 22
swimming 4, 8, 9, 10, 11, 16, 21